Violin **NIKKI IL**
JAZZ ON A WINTER'S NIGHT
11 Christmas classics

Contents

CD track information is given at the top of each piece, in the form 🔘 **1**, 12, with the first (bold) number indicating the full performance track, and the second number the piano-only backing track.

MUSIC DEPARTMENT

OXFORD
UNIVERSITY PRESS

Arranger's note

I was delighted to be asked to work on this great seasonal project and to have the chance to collaborate with the wonderful violinist Ros Stephen, when recording the CD. I'd also like to acknowledge the advice of jazz violinist Dan Oates during the early stages. Each arrangement attempts to capture a different atmosphere, whether it be the warm harmonies by the fireside of 'The Christmas Song' or the sleigh bells ringing in the opening of 'Let it snow!'. The arrangements have been carefully crafted, providing fully notated improvisations and an authentic sound throughout, whether in a folksy or jazz style. This is, I hope, just the starting point for your own interpretations and seasonal creativity.

OXFORD
UNIVERSITY PRESS

Great Clarendon Street, Oxford OX2 6DP,
United Kingdom

Oxford University Press is a department of the University of Oxford.
It furthers the University's aim of excellence in research, scholarship,
and education by publishing worldwide. Oxford is a registered trade mark of
Oxford University Press in the UK and in certain other countries

This collection © Oxford University Press 2014

Nikki Iles has asserted her right under the Copyright, Designs
and Patents Act, 1988, to be identified as the Author of these Works

First published 2014

Impression: 1

ISBN 978–0–19–339344–8

Music origination by Julia Bovee

Printed in Great Britain on acid-free paper by
Halstan & Co. Ltd, Amersham, Bucks.

Credits

Cover illustration by Tony Stephenson © Oxford University Press
Artist photo by Hugh Byrne

The *Violin Jazz on a Winter's Night* CD, featuring Nikki Iles and
Ros Stephen, was recorded at Red Gables Facilities, Greenford, on
11 December 2013. Engineered and co-produced by Ken Blair.
Audio editing by Will Anderson. BMP The Sound Recording Company.

Have yourself a merry little Christmas

words and music
by HUGH MARTIN
and RALPH BLANE
arr. Nikki Iles

inspired by Nat King Cole

Noël nouvelet

trad. French
arr. Nikki Iles

inspired by the John Coltrane Quartet

Let it snow!

words by SAMMY CAHN
music by JULE STYNE
arr. Nikki Iles

inspired by Diana Krall

 tracks **4**, 15

In the bleak mid-winter

words by CHRISTINA ROSSETTI
music by GUSTAV HOLST
arr. Nikki Iles

inspired by Bill Evans

tracks **5**, 16

O little town of Bethlehem

trad. English
arr. Nikki Iles

NIKKI ILES

Violin

JAZZ ON A WINTER'S NIGHT

Piano accompaniment book

Contents

MUSIC DEPARTMENT

OXFORD
UNIVERSITY PRESS

Have yourself a merry little Christmas

words and music
by HUGH MARTIN
and RALPH BLANE
arr. Nikki Iles

inspired by Nat King Cole

Noël nouvelet

trad. French
arr. Nikki Iles

7

inspired by the *John Coltrane Quartet*

10

Let it snow!

words by SAMMY CAHN
music by JULE STYNE
arr. Nikki Iles

* Play bracketed 𝅝 2nd time only.

11

D.S. al Coda

CODA

inspired by Diana Krall

In the bleak mid-winter

words by CHRISTINA ROSSETTI
music by GUSTAV HOLST
arr. Nikki Iles

inspired by Bill Evans

O little town of Bethlehem

trad. English
arr. Nikki Iles

D.S. al Coda

CODA

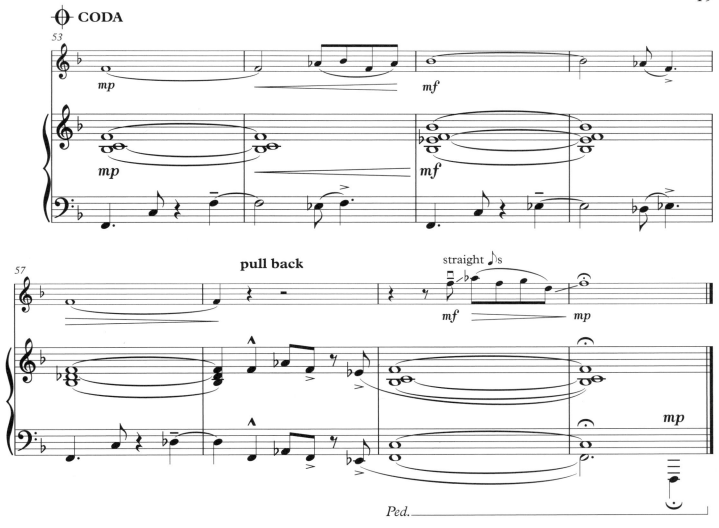

inspired by Vince Mendoza

Balulalow

words 16th century
music by PETER WARLOCK
arr. Nikki Iles

inspired by Norma Winstone

Sans Day Carol

trad. English
arr. Nikki Iles

inspired by Abdullah Ibrahim

Santa Claus is comin' to town

words by HAVEN GILLESPIE
music by J. FRED COOTS
arr. Nikki Iles

'Silent night' has been printed from p.30, after 'Santa Claus is comin' to town', to minimize page turns.

inspired by Paul Bley

Silent night

orig. words by JOSEF MOHR
music by FRANZ XAVER GRUBER
arr. Nikki Iles

32

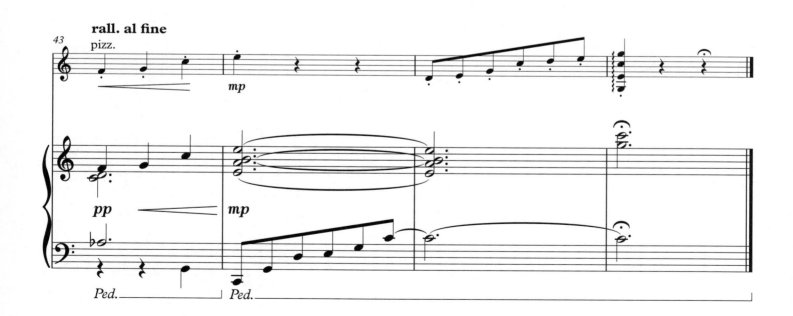

* Alternatively, the piano may take the violin line in this bar, with the violin playing a dotted minim E.

inspired by Thad Jones

Sussex Carol

trad. English
arr. Nikki Iles

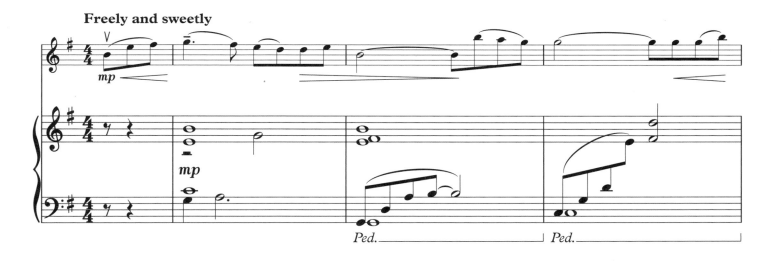

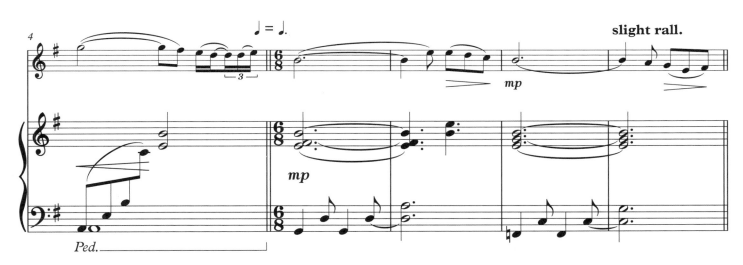

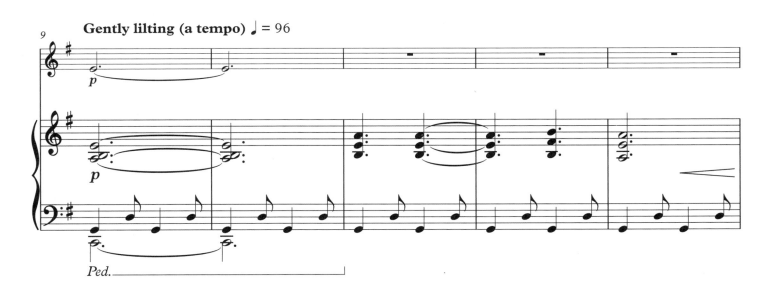

34

inspired by *Richard Rodney Bennett*

The Christmas Song
('Merry Christmas to You')

words and music
by MEL TORMÉ
and ROBERT WELLS
arr. Nikki Iles

* Or:

inspired by Frank Sinatra

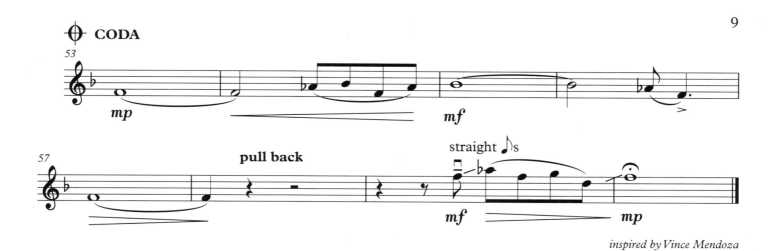

inspired by Vince Mendoza

 tracks **6**, 17

Balulalow

words 16th century
music by PETER WARLOCK
arr. Nikki Iles

inspired by Norma Winstone

Sans Day Carol

trad. English
arr. Nikki Iles

inspired by Abdullah Ibrahim

Silent night

orig. words by JOSEF MOHR
music by FRANZ XAVER GRUBER
arr. Nikki Iles

inspired by Thad Jones

* Alternatively, the piano may take the violin line in this bar, with the violin playing a dotted minim E.

12

Santa Claus is comin' to town

words by HAVEN GILLESPIE
music by J. FRED COOTS
arr. Nikki Iles

inspired by Paul Bley

Sussex Carol

trad. English
arr. Nikki Iles

inspired by Richard Rodney Bennett

tracks **11**, 22

The Christmas Song
('Merry Christmas to You')

words and music
by MEL TORMÉ
and ROBERT WELLS
arr. Nikki Iles

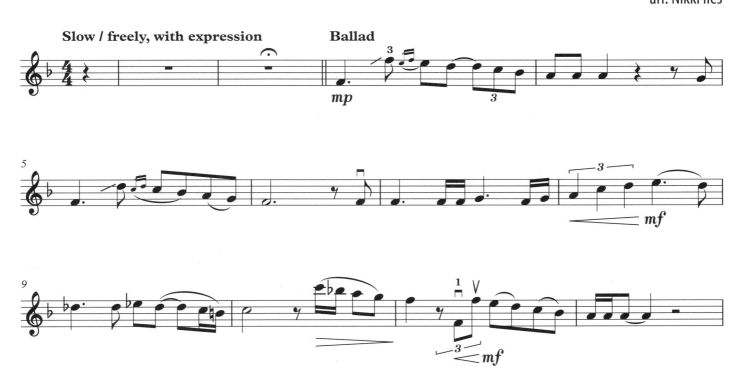

16

inspired by Frank Sinatra